The Cherry

Ruby-Red
Crimson Berry
Luck and Fortune
Fertility Fairy

Silken Blossom
Magic Bloom
Sakura Spirit
Annual Boon

Root and Stem
Fruit to Flower
Celebrate Her
Immortal Power

-Rosemarie

The

TRANSPARENT
WHORE

How I Undressed My Soul

ROSEMARIE

BALBOA.PRESS

A DIVISION OF HAY HOUSE

This book is a work of non-fiction. Unless otherwise noted, the author and the publisher make no explicit guarantees as to the accuracy of the information contained in this book and in some cases, names of people and places have been altered to protect their privacy.

Balboa Press books may be ordered through booksellers or by contacting:

Balboa Press
A Division of Hay House
1663 Liberty Drive
Bloomington, IN 47403
www.balboapress.com
844-682-1282

Print information available on the last page.

ISBN: 978-1-9822-6056-9 (sc)
ISBN: 978-1-9822-6058-3 (hc)
ISBN: 978-1-9822-6057-6 (e)

Library of Congress Control Number: 2020925140

Balboa Press rev. date: 02/18/2021

Dedication

I dedicate the writings in this book to every person that picks it up. To every soul who is ready to take control of their own life and let go of all the shit that isn't theirs to carry. I dedicate this book to myself, my parents, my beloved partner, my children, my brother, my family, Scarlet, my friends, my clients, strangers, and the Universe. I am grateful for all the lessons you have helped me learn in the past and will help me learn in the future. I dedicate my story to your story and the ultimate beauty that you carry inside of you!

A special thank you to Scarlet for being with me through lifetimes past and present. Thank you for being the ultimate supporter in this process of being a writer. Thank you for your endless hours of insight and love as I journeyed through my fears and for your professional advice and positive direct feedback. I adore you and love you too much!

> *"How you do anything, is how you do everything!"*
>
> -Me

Contents

[i carry your heart with me(i carry it in]

i carry your heart with me (i carry it in
my heart) i am never without it (anywhere
i go you go, my dear; and whatever is done
by only me is your doing, my darling)
i fear
no fate (for you are my fate, my sweet) i want
no world (for beautiful you are my world, my true)
and it's you are whatever a moon has always meant
and whatever a sun will always sing is you

here is the deepest secret nobody knows
(here is the root of the root and the bud of the bud
and the sky of the sky of a tree called life; which grows
higher than soul can hope or mind can hide)
and this is the wonder that's keeping the stars apart

i carry your heart (i carry it in my heart)

-E. E. Cummings

Foreword

The year was 2005. For all intents and purposes, I was truly lucky. I had all the markings of a peaceful, if not somewhat boring, small-town life. To the outside world, I had it all.

A loving husband, a beautiful little girl, a cute and cozy first home—I really did have almost everything I needed. Outside, I was smiling. However, inside, I was dying.

I didn't know what was wrong with me or why I genuinely felt like something or someone was missing from my life. I did know that despite being surrounded by beauty in every possible form, I was also so desperately lonely my life felt like a silent, slow-motion, never-ending movie—a never-ending movie with a script someone else was writing.

Little did I know way back in 2005, a script was actually being written. It was a friendship script asked for, prayed about, and co-written with the Spirit. A script designed to bring two beautiful beings back together, out of the depths of their equally lonely and challenging worlds, and into each other's arms. Little did I know this friendship script would drastically and unequivocally change the entire direction and trajectory of my life.

The Universe is a powerful force, my friends. Then again, so is Rosemarie. At the time, I didn't know much about this remarkable, adorable, fascinating young woman. I certainly didn't know she'd been praying for me. I didn't know she'd asked the Universe to send her a friendship so pure and so true it could never be overlooked or denied. I didn't know she wrote a letter, a script of sorts, detailing the very specific qualities and criteria she was hoping to find. I didn't know she could literally hear and feel the Universe pushing her closer and closer to me.

I didn't know what to expect when she showed up on my

doorstep one random Tuesday morning all those years ago. I'm just so very thankful I chose to open the door. With our lives and relationships eerily similar, our daughters the same age, and both of us with a deep, almost yearning desire for connection, my soul instantly recognized Rosemarie's. We've been best friends ever since. We are part of each other's lives because we are supposed to be, we are meant to be, we just cannot not be.

In my own way, I've lived through the pages of this story, too. Over the years, I've seen, I've heard, and I've witnessed the incredible challenges and seemingly insurmountable odds this amazingly beautiful being has dealt with and been through. I know it happened. I was there. Yet, reading this book still gives me pause.

I still can't believe what happened. I still can't believe how it happened. I still can't believe it actually did happen. All of it, everything. Every. Single. Sordid. Detail. When I read the pages of her unbelievable story, I'm reminded of the personal work and universal lessons we are all brought here to work through. When I read the pages of her story, I'm reminded of the greatness of the Spirit, the vastness of the Universe, and the magnificent resilience of the soul. When you read the pages of Rosemarie's story, you just might realize that though your story may be different, your lessons might be the same.

See, here's the thing. You may not be dealing with cancer. You may not be in the midst of complete emotional upheaval after you've completely uprooted your life and left behind everything you've ever known and everything you've ever been conditioned to know. You may not be in the midst of an illicit love affair. You may not be in the midst of yet another, very different kind of love affair. You may not be contemplating or going through a divorce. But you are here for a reason.

Whether for entertainment, a quest for spiritual growth, or just plain morbid curiosity, your soul led you here. To this book. To Rosemarie.

Over the years, I've learned this is a woman who does not hold back. *The way she does anything is the way she does everything.* She commits, she takes on, she tackles, she overcomes. Her story, told through the incredibly honest, raw, sometimes jarring perspective of someone who actually lived it, will undoubtedly touch your heart and hopefully speak to your soul.

You will probably laugh. You will most likely cry. You may even get so angry you end up throwing this sleek, beautiful little book across the room. It's all okay. Just promise me if that happens, you'll eventually pick back up the book and start reading again. I promise you, it's worth it.

In fact, you'll probably read, go back and reread, then reread and read it again because you just cannot believe what you keep on reading! You might not believe someone is brave enough to put her story, this incredible, true story, into words and on paper for the entire world to see. But I know Rosemarie. She's the bravest, sincerest, strongest, most authentic soul I know. She knows her story is meant to help others. That is all that matters.

Rosemarie changed my life. Her friendship changed my world. If you're open and willing to allow it, her story and this book will almost certainly change yours.

-Scarlet

whore:
a person who is regarded as willing to do anything in order to get a particular thing

THE TRANSPARENT WHORE | xv

Preface

All of us have moments of absolute clarity, when a light bulb goes off inside our head. These moments are the ones we don't forget—we can't forget. These moments tend to hit us, wake us, break us, and reshape us. We need them. They create our testimonies and increase our relatability. They are how we connect to other people. They give us awareness. They help us address old limiting beliefs and re-write parts of us that were programmed by others. These moments help us discover our personal TRUTH. They are gifts, not punishments. Each event we experience is an opportunity for our souls to awaken.

My pivotal events of clarity have hit me hard, woken me up, broken me down, and re-shaped me. Through it all, I have found my voice, my truth, and my spiritual foundation. I have set boundaries and learned to love myself, value myself, and say "No." My shakedowns were hard. They hurt, and they made me realize how strong I am and how each day I live is a reflection of me and nobody else.

My soul awoke along the way. These opportunities taught me that life is a practice, that being present and not perfect is true "being." I learned how to be gentle on myself. I learned how to have allowance and acceptance for others. I learned to be slow to criticize and quick to give a hug. I see now that to practice love and kindness, to forgive easily, and to love unconditionally are the ultimate goals.

The following chapters consist of the pain and suffering that resulted in huge amounts of awareness. I am grateful for the suffering. I offer you an intimate window into the hardships I have experienced, wisdom from my journey, faith from my practice, and guidance to perhaps help you along your way—or maybe just an insightful personal testimony that brings you closer to your own inner personal acceptance. We are all somewhere on the continuum of infinity, one soul race. No matter what you're doing to yourself right now, you're still beautiful and worth it!

-Embrace Your Soul Journey!

Somewhere

I have arrived somewhere
And I am not late
I have arrived right here
My perfect fate

I went backwards, and forwards
And upside down
Only to see myself
Flat on the ground

Forwards and backwards
I spun, and I turned
Over and under
To see what I learned

Over and under
I flipped all around
I twisted and turned
To see what I found

Backwards and forwards
I see myself go
Over and under
I finally know

I have arrived somewhere
And I am not late
I have arrived right here
My perfect fate

-Rosemarie

My Awakening

cancer: the disease caused by uncontrolled division of abnormal cells in any part of the body

Tears WERE ROLLING DOWN MY face. I felt horror as I lay paralyzed by the word: *cancer*. I had cancer! I was looking at it with my own eyes on the giant screen in front of me. There it was, a hideous, plum-sized tumor growing inside of my body. I didn't know how this horrible thing had gotten there. Maybe the doctor was wrong, maybe this was all a nightmare and I would wake up.

I was going into shock and felt the spiral of denial. I wanted this to go away. Laying there stark naked, I had never felt more alone and scared. Colon cancer! I was twenty-eight years old—how the fuck did I have colon cancer? The room spun around me, every sound like a dissonant bubble popping in my head. My thoughts were spinning, and I couldn't catch any of them. Then I heard a voice, a voice so loud it jarred me back into the moment. I questioned my sanity, *Am I crazy? Am I completely losing my mind?* The whole room seemed to be elapsing in time, everything a million miles away. But the voice was clear. "Don't worry," I heard it say. "This is only something you have to go through!" Maybe for this voice it was simple and of no concern, but for me, throughout the next year of my life, I would be turned upside-down in order to come right-side-up.

My husband Charlie met me at the hospital. I was in tears

as he wrapped his arms around me. I could feel his heart racing inside his body; we were both terrified at what could come. The GI doc had sent me directly down the road to the community hospital to get a CT scan. I drank some nasty liquid and crawled inside a giant white tube. I couldn't calm my mind; it was soaring from one thought to the next. It was completely out of control.

They were looking for metastasis—other areas of the body that were contaminated by cancer. Had I waited too long to get checked out? Had the cancer split off in all directions, attaching itself to other places inside of me? I had been having unusual symptoms for a few months by then. I'd noticed this weird urgency to go to the bathroom, I had been bleeding and bloating, and I had a constant feeling of fatigue. I knew something wasn't right with me. I had secretly written "**Please Help Me**" on a small white piece of paper and tucked it between two books resting on the shelf in our living room. Had I waited too long? I felt guilty for not taking better care of myself, for not demanding sooner that I see a specialist.

But it wasn't like I'd been ignoring myself; I had gone to see my primary care doctor three times before they referred me. They were focused more on the idea of post-delivery issues. My baby was only four months old when all of this started. I remember the doctor chalking my symptoms up to having a newborn and insisting it was most likely internal hemorrhoids from childbirth. My heart had told me something different, and I knew I needed another opinion. I was so grateful I hadn't given up and kept following my intuition to get rechecked. With my adamant demand, the doctor gave me a referral to see a specialist after three visits over the span of four months.

My husband and I left the hospital in separate cars, hugging each other hard in the parking lot before we left. My drive home was silent. I felt like I was floating outside of my body. I kept seeing the tumor over and over again in my mind. Pulling into my driveway, I wanted to throw up, run away, disappear. I didn't want to face my family. I didn't want something to be wrong with me or for them to worry about me. I felt tightness in my body, a lump in my throat, and sadness pressing against my heart. I wanted everyone in that moment to go away and be sad somewhere else. I don't remember walking into my house that night or how I walked up the stairs. I remember only lying on my living room floor and bleakly staring at the dark green wall. I needed to process, to bargain—I needed just a little time to get it together. I could hear my daughter's sweet voice in the background chatting to my mom and the baby crying. He was hungry. I felt a hand softly touch my back. My brother, with tears in his eyes, said, "I love you, sister." I could feel his worry deep inside of me, and it made me cry too.

I met with Dr. Jamison, my assigned surgeon. He was a reserved man in his late fifties. He was tall and slender with a dry personality. I have to admit, on first meeting him, I wasn't sure he was the right match for me. But then again, I wanted the best surgeon, not a comedian. Dr. Jamison was a straight shooter; he was direct and to the point. He didn't mix his words when he told me this wasn't a clean-cut operation and there was uncertainty involved. I could wake up with a colostomy bag, the cancer could have spread to another organ, the cancer could be in my lymph system—there were many possible risks he couldn't predict. However, Dr. Jamison was hopeful. The CT scan had only shown a bulge in the lower left abdominal area. There were no other areas that appeared contaminated. He admitted to me that he might not be the most sensitive man, but he was the best surgeon for the job and he would take every precaution when he got in there. My initial feeling of uncertainty was replaced with reassurance and trust. His personality was somewhat cold, but his direct and sure nature gave me the confidence I needed. Oddly, at the end of our appointment when he shook my hand, he thanked me for my calm and collected presence. I must have had a dumb look on my face because in my mind I was wondering, *How do other patients act?* Thinking back on that comment, I assume he met with a lot of frantic patients. He was probably used to people who came in hysterical and scared and projected their fear onto him because of their own anger and frustration. I liked that he had thanked me; it strangely made me feel better. It gave me strength to know that he saw strength in me.

The surgery was Monday, leaving me less than three days to prepare myself. Getting my eight-month-old baby to take a bottle and ween him from nursing was at the forefront of my mind. I wanted to keep nursing him; I wasn't ready to let go of that yet, but I knew it was impractical for me to even consider continuing. I would be completely depleted after surgery, and my body would dry up on its own from the lack of stimulation and weight loss. I would be on a special diet following the surgery for weeks. I needed to make peace with weaning him. In the midst of that heartache, I had to start an intense colon prep to completely clean out my system: a couple of gallons of pre-mixed pooping solution. The doctor didn't want any debris at all to lower the risk of infection. I felt myself begin to dig deep into my inner strength. I didn't want to do any of this, but ultimately, I had to do all of it!

There was a strange tension that weekend mixed with lots of love and calls from friends and family who were praying for me, for us. I received an unusual call from an auntie of a childhood friend who said she was led to call me. She said that she had a message for me—that I was an angel, and I was going to be just fine. God had spoken to her and told her I would come out of this perfectly okay. I know that she had been chosen to give me that message, and I needed that phone call.

On Sunday, our pastor came to the house along with my family and Charlie's parents. I was not a religious person but often found myself wanting to be part of spiritual groups. There was a deep part of me that knew there was something we were all connected to. There was an energy, a source of divine love, a power or invisible force that emerged when people came together. I requested a prayer circle in my living room. Everyone sat on the floor in a circle holding hands, and we prayed together. It was a beautiful joining together in the presence of family and friends. As we prayed, I could feel a wave of unconditional love spread around the circle. My heart and soul were content. I surrendered my fear that afternoon in our sacred circle of love. I made a declaration of faith to get well and to trust in the Universe!

Later that evening, I caught myself staring out the bay window at the trees in our front yard. It was a strange moment as I realized the energy all around me. I was uncertain at first as to what it was, but then the overwhelming message flooded my mind. It was the prayers of others. I could actually feel and hear people praying for me. I could hear their words in my head and in the comfort of my body. I heard their names and felt their energy all around me. In that moment, the reason why people were always praying for other people made sense to me. We are all connected to each other and have the ability to send and receive energy through thought and intention.

I held baby Louie in my arms, staring down at his perfect face. I wasn't ready to set him free. I felt betrayed by my body. I wanted to nurse my baby, dammit, not prepare for surgery and give up the sacred time I shared with him. His warm little body was pressed up against mine for the last time. I carefully wrapped him in my arms to embrace every part of him. The green walls of his bedroom were a fortress as we rocked back and forth in our special chair together. We were in our safe space where I always nursed him. He reached up with his hand to grasp my hair and twirl it around his fingers; this was what he did for comfort. I was thinking about how I had made him and that he had grown because of me. I started to cry. I told him I loved him and that he didn't do anything wrong, that Mommy had to get healthy. I wasn't ready to let go, and disappointment continued to wash over me.

Jamison was written in black Sharpie marker on my belly bright and early Monday morning. This was to insure the right doctor would be working on me. I giggled, thinking, *Yeah, I don't want to wake up with one leg instead of a missing colon.* I was in good spirits going into surgery. I had weighed all the facts and gone over every detail in my mind over and over again, and my best option was surgery. There wasn't enough time to heal the tumor naturally, as I was at almost a one hundred percent blockage. The tumor had grown like a rainbow from one side of my colon wall to the other side with a pencil-sized opening left for defecation. I was at a critical point.

Charlie kissed me on the forehead as the nurse came to wheel me into the operating room. I have no memory of the surgery after being told to count backwards from ten. When I woke up five hours later, I was mumbling about a dream.

I was emerging back from some kind of out-of-body experience, a place I had gone during the surgery. I had heard other people talk about having these types of experiences. Maybe there is somewhere all of us go when we have trauma or surgery, a safe, heavenly place our soul transports to for comfort and reassurance while our bodies are worked on. I was wearing a green dress, and there was a tropical flower resting in my hair above my left ear. I was on an island with my family, healthy and well. As the images became clearer, I realized I was attending my brother's wedding. He had recently gotten engaged. I was giving a speech in honor of their love and feeling calm with the knowledge that my cancer was behind me. I awoke from surgery in a state of total peace. What I had experienced, I could only explain as a dream. My brother and husband were staring down at me when I opened my eyes. I tried to tell them I was going to live because I saw myself in the future, but it all came out sounding crazy. In the end, it didn't matter. I knew the message I had been given was meant for me, not anyone else.

There were moments of my recovery where I felt inspired and strong, and then there were moments I felt weak and heavy with fear. It's not easy to recapture the feelings I had during my five-day hospital stay. I kept thinking, *How did this tumor grow inside of me?* The more I asked, the clearer it became that I had needed the tumor in order to awaken into my true self. I had stuffed so many years of emotions into that area of my body that it became toxic with cancer. I had to work on letting go of old conditioning.

On the third night following my surgery, I had a remote reiki session. Reiki is the receiving of unconditional love through universal energy. I had the nurse put a "Do Not Disturb" sign on my door that evening. I didn't want anyone checking my vitals for at least an hour. The morphine line had been taken out that afternoon, and I wanted to start helping my body recover. During my reiki session, I could feel heat and energy rushing up and down my body, small electric currents giving me little jolts of healing. The reiki practitioner told me later that she had lit a candle during our session. She knew the session was over when the candle blew out on its own.

In the middle of that night, I woke to the sound of angels singing to me. Sweat was pouring out of my body; I could feel all the drugs leaving. It was a moment I would never forget and never want to forget—the sound was magical and inexplicable. It was from another world. Their voices were the true sound of angelic healing. Each vibration washed over me again and again until I fell deeply asleep.

Charlie brought the kids into the hospital to visit me. I was surrounded by pink roses and white lilies, flowers of every kind. My room was literally a sea of blooms keeping me company. Charlie handed me a little white piece of paper and said, "I found this tucked between two books on the shelf in the living room." I stared up at him. "When did you write this?" he asked. I told him it had been months ago and felt my eyes begin to well up. He said, "They heard you!" I nodded in gratitude.

I wasn't allowed to leave the hospital until I had walked around the hallways and pooped. I was determined to make it out of bed and down the hallway. To my surprise and everyone else's, I did it. I had passed test one! Test two was a little trickier and more embarrassing, so I'll spare the details. But hey, a poop is a poop. I had my get-out-of-jail card and was heading home.

Before leaving the hospital, I received some good news. My colon margins were clean, and the tumor had been contained, so there was no contamination in my lymph nodes, and the cancer had not metastasized to any other location in my body. This was the best scenario possible and what we had all been crossing our fingers for, waiting to hear.

Oncologist appointments started almost immediately. The first doctor we met with diagnosed the tumor as stage II. He did not recommend chemo and radiation. I had been researching like crazy and had brought with me packets of information on nutrition and healing. I started talking to him about it, and he immediately cut me off. He said that nutrition had nothing to do with my recovery, and I could stop at Burger King on the way home and eat a giant hamburger if I wanted to. Charlie and I were shocked! We looked at each other like, *WTF?* The nutritionist we had seen a week prior had told us the exact opposite information. She'd recommended I eat organic and clean, no red meat at all, drink green tea, and take vitamin D3, turmeric, and B vitamins. *What the hell is this oncologist telling us?* I thought. *Fast food is okay? Next doctor, please.*

We received a recommendation for a female doctor at Hershey Medical Center. We met with her the following week. She was beautiful with dark, shiny hair and lovely almond-shaped eyes. I immediately felt safe with her. She was very thorough and considerate as we went over all of the nutritional information I'd brought. After intently reviewing my hospital reports, she diagnosed the tumor that had been removed as stage III and recommended radiation. This was a graver diagnosis than my initial doctor had given. What the heck? How can one doctor see one thing and another see something else with the same diagnostic report? She also suggested genetic testing because of how young I was. *Mmm, more to think about.*

Oddly, doctor days had become date days for Charlie and I. We would find a cute little cafe or restaurant to have lunch following our appointment and discuss the pros and cons of treatment options. One little spot we found together was just what we needed on that day. It was a sweet refuge that offered a quiet oasis to take our minds away. It was nice to be there with him, but I wish it would have been a normal date instead of a cancer recovery date. No matter how much we enjoyed our date, there was a constant reminder that I was still in this.

My final visit at the first doctor was for a follow-up. Now, he was diagnosing the tumor as stage III and recommending chemo and radiation! I had three months to decide what my plan was. Thank God I had time to decide what to do because everyone had a plan for me, and none were the same. None had been tailored for me by the Universe. The only way to receive that kind of personal plan is to *ask* for yourself. So that is what I started to do.

My first question was about chemo. When I considered saying yes to this question, I would feel horrible. My body was telling me it was a hard *No*. I was learning how to listen. I wasn't opposed to radiation, as I knew that there was only a two-percent chance that I could develop proctitis after I had been radiated. Proctitis is a condition where you cannot control your bowel movements and feel severe urgency to poop. I asked the Universe about the chances of me developing this condition, and the answer I received was *Yes*. The answer came to me with clarity and certainty: I would develop proctitis if I allowed myself to be radiated through the back of my body into the recto-sigmoid area. It would leave me with an incurable condition that I'd have to live with for the rest of my life. Radiation suddenly became a hard-fucking *No*!

I had mixed feelings about genetic testing. Did I need to know the results of this? I wasn't sure I wanted to know. Once you know something, you can't unknow it! How would the new knowledge affect me? I <u>asked</u> the Universe about this and heard very clearly in reply: *That one is up to you! It doesn't change anything for you. You are cancer free, and DNA can be healed.* I was shocked to hear this. DNA can be healed? I was fascinated by this new truth. I had the genetic testing done and tested positive for one of the four genes, the one that caused the least amount of concern for the doctors. I was excited to work on healing my own DNA.

I had eliminated dairy, gluten, sugar, most grains, and all red meat. I replaced all my self-care products with chemical-free organic ones and began to use intuition to navigate every decision I made. I was on a mission, and my motive was not to die! I felt a calling deep inside of me. I felt inspiration from another dimension, something I never felt before, a super-human strength that motivated me. It gave me the power to continue to conquer and a reason to live. I surrendered myself in meditation daily to the Universe. I knew I would never be the same.

Twelve weeks sped by on the fast track to recovery after my surgery. I had reclaimed my body. I was feeling strong and adjusting to my new lifestyle choices. This big change was an exhausting process for Charlie and me. I didn't feel supported. Charlie wanted everything to go back to how it had been before cancer. That was impossible. I would never be the same. He wasn't really on board with my *I-heard-it-from-the-Universe* technique. I wanted him to align with me on a spiritual level. A lot was coming up for me emotionally, and I didn't completely understand what was happening. Looking back, I realize I was growing out of who I'd been trained to be and into who I was here to be. I was changing in vibration, and those who knew the old me were confused. I remember standing in our kitchen one night, yelling, "I'm doing this with you or without you! But I'm doing this, so get the fuck out of my way!" I was so angry with Charlie at that moment. I was angry with him for not changing too. I was angry with him for his insensitivity, for not initiating anything, for wanting me to do chemo, and for being scared. I was just so angry. It was the first time I can remember standing in my power, standing up for myself, and being one hundred percent fine if he didn't support me. In fact, I was fine if nobody supported me. Cancer brought something out in me. It had awoken the inner tigress in me, and it truly felt amazing. I was changing!

The dreaded call with the oncologist was approaching fast. He was waiting patiently for my answer on whether or not to start chemo. My life seemed to be full of big decisions. The choice to start chemo was particularly daunting. It was a decision I knew my own answer to, the answer that was right for me, but it went against everyone else's opinion.

A couple of days leading up to the call, I reached out to my mom and my friend Tiva. I trusted my mom and Tiva to <u>ask</u> the Universe on my behalf for insight in regard to a healing path. I told them the decision I had made and what I needed them to help me with. I <u>asked</u> them both to pray for me and listen to what the Universe had to say. They both agreed to help me. I went to bed that night with a feeling of great peace. Both of them called me the following morning with news to share. Tiva revealed to me the vision she had been given in her meditation. She said that she had seen a beautiful white lotus being placed into my second chakra. Chakras are energy centers of spiritual power within the human body. The second chakra is located two fingers below the belly button. It is called the Sacral Chakra. It represents personal acceptance and boundaries, two areas I needed to work on. I could feel the white lotus inside of me. I intuitively knew she was speaking the truth. The lotus flower has a spiritual meaning of purity and rebirth.

White Lotus Flower

OM Mani Padme Hum. Praise to the Jewel in the Lotus.
The white lotus flower awakened within
The awakening has begun
I can feel her growing
She is emerging through the mud
The awakening has begun
Her bloom has started its ascension...
She is renewed
The awakening has begun
Inspiration rising inside
Energy from the root of being
The awakening has begun.

-Rosemarie

My mom received her message through a dream she'd had the night before. She started by saying how scared she was for me and that she loved me and that because of her own fear, she wanted me to take the chemo and radiation. But she also knew I was a spiritual woman who followed the guidance of the Universe. As she spoke, I felt goosebumps raise up all over my body. This was confirmation that she was about to share the truth with me. "Honey, in my dream you were walking up a beautiful spiral staircase in a white flowing gown. All of our deceased loved ones were standing around the staircase. As I looked at each of their faces, they were all shaking their heads and yelling, *No! Don't let her take the treatment, she is fine, she doesn't need it!*" My mom knew the decision that message would solidify for me. I thanked her for her faithful prayer. It confirmed what my own heart had already told me.

When the doctor called me later that afternoon, he asked me if I was ready to start treatment. I informed him that I was not going to receive any chemo or radiation. He uttered back, "What?" in shocked amazement. "Why not? Every young person takes the treatment." I gently thanked him for his advice, offered my respect to his medical position, but ended with my truth. I let him know that I had prayed to the master of My Universe, and it was a firm *No* for me. He couldn't believe it and wished me luck.

I was committed to healing and doing whatever it took to never create cancer again. I was going to **Ask, Surrender, Receive,** and **Take Action**, even if it didn't make sense to anyone else.

From there, I let the Universe take over again. I began my conversation with the Universe, confessing I had declined treatment and that I was scared but in total trust of the guidance I had been shown and given. I _asked_ for more help and for more guidance. I _asked_ for something to stabilize my system and detoxify my body.

"Pectin! Pectin! Pectin!" That was the word I woke up to the morning after I prayed for a plan to stabilize and detox my body.

It was unmistakable. The voice I heard was so loud and direct it abruptly woke me from my sleep. I looked over at Charlie, assuming he was talking in his slumber. But he was deeply nested into the blankets, soundly sleeping, and not making a noise. I accepted the auspicious sign from the Universe and made my way out into the dining room to Google *pectin* on the computer. First, Google led me to the definition of pectin as a gelling agent for jam. That couldn't be right. I heard the voice again telling me to rephrase my question. I Googled *pectin* and *cancer*. There it was, *modified citrus pectin*. There was an article on how modified citrus pectin goes into the body, attaches to free radical cells, deactivates them, and flushes the cells out of the body. *What?* I bought it. I took it twice a day, followed a new diet plan, and developed new thinking patterns and a new appreciation for my life. It was amazing how every question I *asked* the Universe was answered. All I had to do was *ask*. I declared to the Universe that I was done being someone else. I declared that I would stop being the people pleaser, the middleman, the good one, the safe bet. I declared that I was ready to step into my life.

Cancer changed me. Facing my mortality changed me. I began to question everything that I had ever been taught by my parents, preachers and teachers, my relatives, friends, my husband, and every single influence that I could think of. It was as if a veil was being lifted from my eyes. So many things I had been told by others started to feel like utter bullshit. I had been birthed into a relationship with my higher self, my soul. She was loud and fierce and was done being kept in a heart-shaped box. She was tired of playing small; she wanted to be the lioness, not the mouse.

Set Sail

The mast rose up
Till it hit the sky
My heart fell open
As the tide pulled high

The ocean water crashed
While the ship held strong
My heart fell open
As the tide went wrong

The wheel turned hard
Catching its course
My heart fell open
As the tide held force

The ocean water calmed
And the ship set sail
My heart fell open
As the tide went frail

My heart fell open
As I set sail!

-Rosemarie

My Lesson: Dis-ease

CANCER WAS BIG ENOUGH TO get my attention. I had manifested something scary enough to wake myself up! Before cancer, I hadn't been living in my true power. I had been keeping myself small. I had been living out of the conditioning that had been created for me rather than becoming the woman I wanted to be. Disease taught me that everything is connected. That energy follows thoughts and that the thoughts I was allowing no longer served me. I learned how to identify these thoughts and weed from my subconscious the people-pleaser seeds that had been deeply planted. I learned how to say *No* and to have a voice of my own. I recognized that getting attention from other people through my own self-sacrifice had created disease within me. I realized the power of surrender and the power in _asking_ the Universe for help and guidance. There was power in _asking_! Cancer taught me how to be powerful and brave!

The Move

move: a change of place, position, or state

"You can't heal in the same environment that made you sick!"

-Me

TWO MONTHS HAD PASSED AFTER my surgery, and I needed a break. Mom and I booked tickets to Arizona for a long weekend to visit my brother and his fiancé. I was excited to get away after all the craziness of the previous year with the new baby, cancer, surgery, and intense recovery. I had always dreamed about living in Arizona. Charlie and I had discussed moving there shortly after getting married but had aborted the idea pretty quickly. We honestly hadn't been brave enough to leave our small town and create a life of our own at that time. Now was my chance to experience Arizona and see if I liked it.

I couldn't shake the feeling that my visit to Arizona would offer another piece to my spiritual puzzle. I could feel it in my bones that there was someone there I had to meet. I searched online for intuitive healing, and Sedona popped up. Intrigued and excited, I scrolled down the page until Naomi's name literally jumped out at me. I was immediately drawn to the energy of her website. I sent a request via her scheduling page to book a session.

Her response offered an opening that aligned perfectly with my upcoming trip. Of course, it did. I booked it!

The drive into Sedona took my breath away. I was mesmerized by the rock torrents that resembled red rock castles in the sky. I was in love! I felt at home in Arizona, like there was an expansion of energy there that gave me an opportunity to grow. I could feel it momentarily wash away the small-town programming that had been built into each cell of my being. Lancaster, Pennsylvania, is a beautiful landscape with majestic farmland, rolling hills, quaint covered bridges, and old-fashioned ways of living. It was a safe and simple place to grow up. However, there was a harsh conservatism that filtered through the area. It had a strong religious undertone that felt restrictive and unsupportive. I was a spiritual, intuitive liberal living inside a beautiful prison. Arizona immediately allowed me to see there was no door on my cage after all; I felt free to jump out and dance in the desert.

I excitedly arrived at my appointment, and Naomi met me at the door. I wasn't sure what to expect and was a little nervous, but I was ready to receive what the Universe had planned for me that day. Naomi was a non-threatening, small lady with tiny facial features and long black hair that went to her waistline. She was in her mid-forties and had mild lines at the corners of her eyes, revealing her age. Her voice was soft. She asked me my intention for our session together, and I told her that I was open to receiving whatever came through. Naomi gave me a body massage while she intuitively channeled information from my guides and loved ones on the other side. She began by connecting her energy to my team of messengers, those who were there to work with me that day. She slowly started telling me personal things about my family and Charlie. She knew he was a singer and had a powerful and strong voice. Naomi could see that I was healthy now and there was no more cancer in my body. She mentioned my DNA was healing. I could feel her using energy work on me like reiki, and she sent various colors into my body. I felt releases everywhere and experienced tiny waves of energy as she spoke lovingly about my life and the directions it could go in. There were moments when emotion welled up in me, and as I exhaled, I could feel the deep release of these stored emotions. My session with Naomi was everything I had been expecting. It gave me additional peace of mind and was another divine experience to add to my collection of confirmations.

The trip to Arizona went by quickly. Before I knew it, I was on the drive home from the Philadelphia airport. I was sitting in the backseat with my eyes closed as my mom and stepdad chatted in the front. I had gotten into meditation and visualization since being diagnosed with cancer and was taking a few minutes to breathe and connect. As I was moving my focus in and up, I felt a presence come all around me and saw a beautiful woman come into my mind. She was holding out both of her hands to me. I was so overcome I felt tears on my cheeks; they were rolling out of my eyes with joy as I received this unconditional feeling of pure love. I had absolutely no idea who this woman was. She looked like a goddess, holding one hand up and the other hand out. I soon learned it was Kuan Yin, the goddess of unconditional love and compassion. I was so humbled to have this visitation with her during my meditation. She quickly became my favorite meditation guide. I called upon her unconditional love often.

Three Months Later

The air was blowing through my hair as Charlie and I zoomed up I-17 North to Sedona in our cherry red convertible. I watched Charlie's face light up as we drove into Sedona. His eyes focused on the same red rock castles I had fallen in love with a few short months before. We drove around town all day, stopping to take pictures and go shopping. As we ate lunch overlooking the gorgeous red rocks, our conversation drifted to our move to Arizona. We discussed how we would do it, where we would live, how we would tell our family, and when would be a good time to make the transition. It was a dream come true. I could literally feel a line connecting two dots on our soul charts. This was really going to happen—we were really going to move three thousand miles away and start a new chapter of life together in the desert.

The decision to move seemed so easy when we were sitting in that little restaurant in Sedona. So why was it so hard to tell our family? There was such a mixture of excitement and disappointment as we announced our plans to auction off our house and move to Arizona in ten months. We both felt shame and guilt. We were selling Charlie's family home, and it felt like we were betraying the generosity his mom had given us. Each of Charlie's brothers had had the opportunity to buy the house from his mom. She had offered each of them the same deal. The oldest brother, Rudy, lived there for many years and decided to move out when he and his girlfriend wanted to buy their own house. They wanted something of their own without all the memories and attachment of the family home. Charlie's brother Sam had died in the woods behind the house in a hunting accident when they were kids. It had been devastating for their family. Charlie had told me about the hardship that Sam's death had put on the family. He told me the heartache from losing a child wasn't something they had ever been truly able to recover from. Charlie's parents divorced, leaving the family in more trauma and devastation. Time calmed the pain within the family but couldn't heal the wound it had carved. The youngest brother, Alex, had moved into the house, and Charlie would live there when he was on break from college and then after he graduated. Eventually, Alex moved out with his fiancé. When I met Charlie, he was living in the house as a bachelor. We dated and fell in love fast, and soon I was living in the house, too. We lived there together and paid rent until we were married and ready to buy the house from his mom. There was no written agreement that we couldn't sell the house in the future. When his family found out we were moving, it was hard.

Words were spoken that were not kind. I understood, though—the house carried heavy memories, and it was hard to let that go. For Charlie and I, it was time to move on.

There was a lot of preparation needed over the following months in order to get the house ready: laying new tile, painting, and fixing the leaky sinks that had dripped for years. Why are leaky sinks always important enough to fix for someone else? It was a lot of work, but we kept our eye on our goal of sunny Arizona.

Our families gathered outside of our house the morning of the auction. Some were there to support us, and others were being nosy, as they didn't agree with our decision to sell the family home. The house went up for auction, and back and forth the auctioneer went. I felt like I was on a carnival ride going up and down as the price climbed higher. Nerve-wracking excitement filled my body as I crossed my fingers for the highest selling price possible. Then "Sold!" rang through the air. A sigh of relief left my body as I wrapped my arms around Charlie's neck. *Holy shit, we're moving!*

The transition could not have been smoother. We had put it out there that we needed housing, and what seemed like only a few days later, my brother called us with great news: the house beside him and my sister-in-law would be coming up for rent. The man who lived there was buying a house and wanted out of his lease. Could it get any more perfect for us? Here we were, moving across the country to Arizona where we knew no one except my brother and his wife, and we were going to live right next door to them. The house was absolutely perfect and in walking distance to the elementary school where Rosebud would be attending.

The permanent house hunt began: we hired a realtor, created a list of things we wanted in a house, and started to <u>ask</u> for our house to present itself in divine timing. We arrived in Arizona on November 18, and by February 2, my 30th birthday, we were sitting in the mortgage office signing all the paperwork to our new house! It was thrilling.

At first, life was exhilarating. We had new territory to explore. Our adventures included beautiful drives north to Sedona or Flagstaff and scenic excursions south to Tuscan. Everything was new and exciting; even the grocery store had its own flare. Weekends became our official time to hike new trails, experience local restaurants, and get a feel for our new home. It was fun and freeing to be somewhere else.

Time, however, brought back the truth that we were three thousand miles away from everything familiar. I started to develop home sickness!

I missed my best friend Scarlet and our religious Tuesday playdates. Every week for almost five years, we alternated Tuesdays, spending one at my house and the next at hers. She wasn't just my best friend, she was my ultimate confidant. I shared everything with her. It was abundantly clear to me that our connection in this life was not the beginning of our friendship but rather a continuation of our souls from many lifetimes together.

I intentionally met Scarlet when my daughter Rosebud was eighteen months old. I was experiencing my first round of loneliness and noticed my soul calling out for friendship. The idea to pray for a best friend to come into my life flooded my mind. So that is exactly what I did. I wrote a prayer to the Universe stating my desire for someone amazing and exquisite to fill the void that I was feeling. Shortly after that prayer was sent out, her name popped into my head. See, I already knew her but didn't *know* her. Our husbands had coached soccer together, and we happened to have babies at the same time. Because she wasn't my direct acquaintance, her name only dawned on me after the prayer was sent out—after I had _asked_ for her. What happened following that prayer was nothing short of miraculous. And in Arizona, I missed her.

I also longed for my grandparents, whom I'd visited every Wednesday morning. They loved seeing the kids; it was the highlight of their week, and we had weekly rituals with them. My nanny saved old bread to feed the ducks. The duck pond was only a short distance from their house, so we would walk there. After the duck pond, we would eat lunch at their house and often follow lunch with a drive to McDonalds for caramel sundaes. My nanny was a darling to us, and my pe-paw was a big friendly man whom I considered another best friend. He made me feel so special and loved. We had inside jokes together, and I would often tell him he was my favorite. I missed them, too!

Charlie was playing gigs three to four nights a week on top of his full-time job to provide us with a comfortable lifestyle as he worked on his draw. A draw is an advance against future compensation from commission payments. Charlie owed thousands of dollars to his company. He was responsible for making up that money in sales commissions. Eventually, this would allow him a platform for growth. It put an enormous amount of stress on him to make up that money in a down market and in an area of work that he was unfamiliar with. I knew he was struggling, but I had so much of my own pain surfacing that I couldn't be strong for him anymore. I certainly didn't want to hear one more conversation about the office and how *so-and-so* wasn't doing *whatever*! I wanted to be supportive of Charlie, I truly did, but the hamster wheel started to feel like the movie *Groundhog Day*!

I understood why he was out gigging, but that didn't stop my resentment from slowly growing. It was lonely being at home with two little kids all the time without having a solid friend group or family around to support me. I could feel the resentment turning into anger as the months passed by, and a wall began building itself around me.

Cancer had awoken my inner lioness, but she was far from healed. I wasn't really experiencing any joy, and I was falling out of love with Charlie. Our life together was becoming too predictable. I felt like I was missing out on something, that I wasn't really living the life I wanted with him. To be honest, I really didn't know myself. In the back of my mind, I thought about leaving Charlie.

In an attempt to escape, I began having lucid dreams about being with other men. It felt like I was living two lives: one with Charlie and the kids as a lonely stay-at-home wife and mother, and another where I was being ravaged and adored by night. It was crazy. I didn't like it, but I didn't know how to stop it. I felt very unsatisfied, and I began to notice something very unhappy developing in my marriage. The lonelier I got, the more distant I became. I noticed I was becoming critical of Charlie and starting to believe he couldn't do anything right. I saw him become tense and walk on eggshells around me. He started drinking more often, both at home and when he played at his gigs. The worst new behavior Charlie developed was when he would drive home drunk after his gigs. I felt him escaping, too. Not in his dreams like me, but through alcohol. He had his own pressures. Moving hadn't been easy for him; he had no family in Arizona, no friends, and a new job that was draining his life force.

Our life was busy, so I had plenty of distractions to take my mind off of my loneliness. I was a master at disguising my true feelings, anyway, so life went on as usual. I enrolled in a two-year holistic nutrition and coaching program to enhance my own resume. It was something I'd had on my mind before moving. It certainly took up enough time and kept me pleasantly occupied. But when it ended, I returned right back to my loneliness.

My saving grace was a small group of beautiful women. They were all moms with little kids who were looking for a connection. We started meeting once or twice every month. I would describe us as spiritual misfits who talked about metaphysics and everything "woo-woo." We ate lunch together, worked on artwork, and talked about and practiced our intuitive abilities. They saved a part of me from dying. I was inspired by them, and being with them gave me the confidence to believe in my spiritual gifts.

As my life went on, I became really good at receiving intuitive messages. Information just came to me effortlessly. Before I knew it, clients were being referred to me, and I was booking sessions. It felt like the next natural step for me to take. I was a practicing massage therapist for many years of my early life. Over the course of that work, I had accumulated certifications in reiki, intuitive energy healing, essential oils, crystals, holistic nutrition counseling, and spiritual coaching.

Word was spreading fast about my intuitive gifts, so much so that I outgrew seeing clients from home and began praying for office space. My first step in anything that I do is to _ask_. So I wrote a detailed letter to the Universe stating my desire for an office. I was specific in what I <u>asked</u> for, right down to the details of working alongside a psychologist. I had it in my mind that a psychologist would be a perfect fit for me because of the amount of information I received to elevate personal growth. I surrendered the letter and let it go. Not even a month later, I was in Sedona attending a Past Life Regression Certification course when I met a lovely blonde-haired lady. We immediately hit it off.

Strategically, she began to inquire about me. I told her I was an intuitive consultant and looking for a shared office space working alongside a psychologist. No sooner had the words left my mouth when she announced that she herself was a psychologist, and her current office had a space available for rent. In that moment, the air stopped moving, time stood still, and tears fell from my eyes. My letter had been received; the Universe had read it and aligned me with this angel.

Charlie didn't really understand what I did with my clients. He had been brought up strictly Lutheran and had a strong program around religion and his beliefs. One night, he was so belligerent he yelled out at me, "You and your spiritual fucking bullshit!" It was painful and hurt me, but it wasn't an unfamiliar feeling. My emotional skin had fashioned itself out of leather by this stage of our relationship. The intended cut gave me momentum to fight harder for myself and keep running on my path. I was in the infantile stage of my awakening. I had only just begun identifying my own patterns and wounds, and I had just barely become brave enough to notice my shadow.

> *"The desert is a funny place. It's an alcove to heal. There is a beckoning that calls you deep into your soul work! It illuminates your wounds and mirrors your shadow, and like a serial killer, you face one old condition after another."*
>
> *-Me*

I had identified a very deep bullet hole from my childhood—the aftermath of the affair that had broken up our family and led to my parents' divorce. I still felt the pain of my parents' separate households and the destruction of a family who had once loved each other. I was fourteen years old looking across the table at my twelve-year-old brother when the news floated out of our parents' mouths and into our innocent ears. The air suddenly became stale with truth: they were breaking up, they didn't love each other anymore, they wanted out of the cocoon they themselves had spun. I wasn't ready to be a butterfly yet, I didn't want to grow up so fast, I liked it in our cocoon, I was safe there. I felt robbed of every potential I would never see. My parents broke up.

I went from a straight-A honor student and president of my class to an untamable wild and free spirit. I found my way through five difficult years, most of which I can't remember, stuffing fistfuls of heartache into the core of my being.

And now, I could feel my closely protected hurt rising to the surface of my life as I looked at Charlie with hatred. I felt the pattern of my conditioning swirl around inside of me; like a python, it had swallowed me whole. I was ready to create my own affair, my own exit out of this suffocating, dead marriage.

Wake Me

It's no big secret
What you do to me at night
I can't stop falling
Deep into the fight

You keep kissing
All the parts of me that hide
I keep finding
All the pieces kept inside

Wake me from this dream
That clutches at my heart
Take away my fear
And tear me apart!

-Rosemarie

My Lesson: Conditioning

THE MOVE TO ARIZONA TAUGHT me that just because I had an Awakening through *dis-ease*, I was far from healed. I learned that I had layered myself with stories that were no longer serving me. Moving to Arizona tore away the wrapping paper and exposed my shadow, allowing me to see what I had been hiding. It gave me permission to begin the process of letting go. All of the conditioning that had been programmed in me was free to fall away. My bad habit of shoving how I felt deep down inside me didn't work anymore. I couldn't hide my anger and sadness anymore. It was coming out on its own, no matter how hard I tried to cover it up. My stories were only an illusion of the truth that I was getting ready to face.

> *"When a person reaches a place of despair, they get into a position to face their shadow."*
>
> -Me

The Breakdown

breakdown: a failure of relationship or system

"A truth is formed by experience."

-Me

IT WAS NEW YEAR'S EVE, and only moments before, we had agreed to leave the party, as the evening was getting late. The kids were falling asleep on the floor, and my parents were ready to get home.

In the following moment, I felt as if the room had fallen away. I stood alone with my head tilted to one side, watching Charlie in disbelief. The full moon shone its light down and illuminated the truth right in front of me. My heart drowned while I watched Charlie drift off into the night air, leaving me stranded again to pick up the pieces. He grabbed four beers from the cooler and headed to the end of the yard where the firepit burned high. My stomach turned as he took a seat next to his buddy and handed him two of the beers he had been carrying. I wanted to kill him.

I could feel something snap inside of me. A deep feeling of hate rose up in my body. I was done, it was over, I was not going to feel this way one more fucking day. I refused to keep hearing myself tell the same frustrated, annoying story over and over again. This is not what I wanted. I was at the pivotal point of no return. Clarity hit me, infiltrated my body like a virus, and shook my soul. I finally realized I was dying in this relationship.

One week earlier…

It was Christmas 2014, and I did the only thing I could think of doing at that moment. I screamed out to the Universe for help. *Are you fucking listening to me? I am desperate, broken, and defeated. This is my emergency!* I hit my knees in surrender and made that 911 prayer to the Universe. *God, please send me another man! A man who will honor and respect me. A man who will love me and make me feel beautiful. Send me a man who will listen to me and hear me. Send me someone that takes this pain away!* I was desperate.

That was my prayer. That was the moment when everything began to shift. It didn't shift in the holy, sweet, heavenly way I would have imagined. It was more along the lines of, *Holy shit, what the fuck just happened to my life?*

When you hear that the Universe works in mysterious ways, this is not a lie—*it works in mysterious ways.* It will honor us in our darkest hours as we make our own choices—as fucked as they may be—and let us fall headfirst into our desperate shadows.

I wanted out of my life. I wanted to know that I was not going to spend the rest of it with the man I had married. I hated him. My prayer was perfect, and it was surely desperate enough to get Charlie's attention. Lying face to face, I blurted it out—I told him what I had prayed for. I was sure I'd get some kind of reaction. It was obvious I was calling out for attention, that I was so fucking unhappy I had prayed for another man to come into my life.

In response, he just looked at me and said nothing. *Nothing.* How could he not hear me? His wife of fifteen years had looked him square in the face and told him she just prayed to God to be sent another man because she hated his fucking guts, and he said absolutely nothing? His blank stare cut into my heart. What was he, a deaf robot?

At this point, I had convinced myself that I didn't like the way he kissed me or the way he touched me. We disagreed on everything. If I said "white," he said "black." I blatantly thought his point of view sucked. I didn't respect him; in fact, I thought he was an argumentative moron. I avoided him and shared nothing too personal, revealing, or deep about myself. I was afraid to share; my wounds were too raw. I knew he would go right for my jugular and leave me no time to recover. He loved to throw me under the bus while making himself look good like he was some kind of hero. I had become a joke to him with my spiritual practice. Everything I believed in was my "spiritual fucking bullshit." He was a dick. He was mean and would say whatever he could think of to hurt me in those moments. I was so fucking pissed at him for trapping me in this horrible life. I had no sparkle left. I could feel my magic fading away. I could feel my soul heading out the door. I hated him for not giving a shit about me and for not even trying to stop me from having an affair. I had admitted my intention to fuck someone else, I had told him I was praying for another man to come into my life—who says nothing to that? Who would just stare blankly at the person they loved and not respond to a nuclear statement like, "I prayed for someone else to come into my life"? He could have tried to stop me. Anything would have been better than nothing. I hated him. I hated everything about him. I was totally disconnected. I cut my heart strings, the strings that had bound us together. I energetically left our marriage. I accepted that my marriage was over. I didn't know how or when it would end, but I knew it was going to.

Hell

What tortures souls beyond despair
Are the crimson windows of a foes bent glare,
The haze of moonlight on a breaking dawn
Or the tinge of sadness of a love far gone.

Echoing terrors of taverns untold
Of a young love used, bought, and sold.
The ripping ache of a beautiful liar,
Burnt again-raw flesh to the fire.

Forgive me for sounding so broken and torn,
But the good lord never promises perfection when born.
Bruised, and battered, and feeling quite poor,
The Devil quickly began checking his score.

Four to the good and ten to the bad,
"Silly little bitch you're almost had!"
But the devil underestimated all of my wit,
In light of my broken heart, I will not quite.

Bolts of lightning crashed all around,
Still no sign of a hell bound found.
The Devil threw up his lance in a rage,
Screaming "Find me that bitch, she belongs in my cage!"

The people scurried in a crazed, mad manic,
But I had escaped leaving the devil in panic.
I still see the haze of the moonlit air
On cold lonely nights when no one is there.

-Rosemarie

My Lesson: Desperation

I WAS A DESPERATE, BROKEN WOMAN, wife, and mother of two. I felt empty and alone and lived every day hoping someone would rescue me from my life. I wanted the fantasy. I wanted the affair. I wanted a handsome knight in shining armor to ride into my life and rescue me from the hell I was living. I wanted out! I wanted to abandon my life with Charlie and the kids and create something new. In my twisted, conditioned mind, my feelings were normal. Divorced parents had been my own experience at fourteen. My family had been broken by an affair for the hope of something better. I watched the fantasy ruin our family. I watched the cowardliness dissolve the love between my parents. Deep inside, I knew it didn't work, but I couldn't escape the conditioning of what I had experienced as a child.

I learned that God listens to our hearts with support and unconditional love. God is the Universe, God is the source. Faith is our responsibility; when we lack faith, we miss the big picture. We act out, we get angry, we hate, and we pray frustrated, selfish prayers. We behave in ways that lack integrity and consideration for others. I did this. I hurt other people, even the ones I had vowed to love the most in this lifetime. I got desperate instead of dedicated.

The Affair

affair: a romantic or passionate attachment, typically of limited duration

IN JANUARY 2015, I HELD my breath as I shook hands with what was, at the time, only a stranger. I felt electricity move between us as his gaze looked me up and down. Butterflies rushed through my body, and a rusty light flickered on inside of me. I felt the affair begin….

John was like a character from a movie. He was older and foreign and handsome, and he walked like he owned the world. I met John in the park on a beautiful, ordinary afternoon. I threw a baseball to my son, who was smiling across the field at me. He threw the ball back. We had only been playing a few minutes when we were joined by a little boy. Trailing behind him was his dad. It felt like time froze as this man walked toward me. I knew I was in trouble! I instantly remembered the prayer I had sent out, my cry for help. *Could this be the man I prayed for?*

We made appropriate small talk with each other—nothing out of the ordinary, just two parents watching their kids play. It all seemed innocent. I asked him if he was married; he wasn't. When I told him I was, instant disappointment crossed his face. There was an obvious mutual chemistry between us; it was bouncing back and forth like a ping pong ball. I felt myself blushing as he politely told me I was beautiful. I wanted more. *Give me more.*

In my head flashed a scene from a novel I had read: a desperate, young housewife being seduced and pulled close by a handsome stranger in the park, time standing still as they slowly fell into each other on the grassy bank. I had a full-blown case of fantasy adultery. No one could prove a mental affair. *Right?* I was still safe; I hadn't done anything wrong. I walked away that day telling myself it had only been an innocent flirtation at the park.

Nothing was changing at home. Charlie and I continued to struggle day after day, and I had stopped sleeping with him. I was no longer interested in the one thing that was good between us and kept us connected. I was totally checked out. I was living from day to day playing house. I kept thinking, *This can't be the rest of my life. I am only thirty-four years old. Please, Universe, I need to be plugged back in, I want to feel again. I wanted to be ravished on the grassy banks of that park.*

I had forgotten about my stranger. I honestly never expected to see him again. But as fate would have it, I was wrong. To my surprise and delight, I saw him two weeks later at the same park on another ordinary afternoon. There was a sparkle in his shimmery blue eyes as he confidently approached me. I felt excited as I gave him a quick and friendly hug hello. We were easy together. Our conversation flowed like honey, as if we had known each other a hundred years. I saw him everyday after school in the park. It was an unspoken promise we had made to each other without ever saying a word. I could feel life coming back to me. I confided in him my unhappiness in my marriage and how I had prayed for the Universe to bring someone else into my life. He understood when I talked about the Universe. He didn't make fun of me; instead, he shared how the Universe worked in his life, too. He had been through a lot and believed in <u>asking</u> the Universe for help. We soon became fast friends. I was falling in love with this stranger at the park. He listened to me, he gave me advice and attention, he spoke the same language as me. Most importantly, we connected on a deep and spiritual level. He knew exactly what to say to get into my head.

We were park friends. I could have left it at that. I could have just stayed friends with him. But I didn't...I was too curious and already emotionally connected. I loved him. I felt beautiful and inspired around him. A slow and steady friendship had been building between us. I trusted him.

We had outgrown our park meetings and met for coffee one morning. It was different being alone with John. We didn't have to juggle our conversation and play with the kids. We were alone. *Oh my God, we were alone!* We talked for hours, walking and holding hands, enjoying the quiet of just us. I knew I had crossed a line. I knew I was in danger. I didn't care—I didn't care what happened to me or my marriage. I didn't care because a light had turned on so brightly inside of me, and I felt alive again. Our coffee date ended with a kiss so passionate I felt like a starstruck teenager with my body awakening in every direction as I fell deep into the infidelity. I liked it, I liked the intensity, I liked the betrayal and secrecy of it all. I had no regard for what I was doing. I was a prisoner who had been set free and was finally enjoying life after years of being caged.

The Kiss

I wasn't looking when he found me
I simply thought, can he see me?
I wasn't seeking when he saw me
I simply thought, how can this be?
I wasn't hoping when he touched me
I simply thought, he holds the key
I wasn't breathing when he kissed me
I simply felt him set me free!

-Rosemarie

I crossed the bridge of no return with John. I found myself naked in his bed one afternoon, intertwined with his body. He moved my hair back away from my face as he looked closely at me. It felt like time had frozen for a moment, creating a snapshot and automatically adding its imprint to my infinite memory. This became a refuge to escape in. He became my secret sanctuary. Our intimate times together were intense and passionate, including our conversations, which seemed to move gracefully from one topic to the next. It was easy to share with him. I never felt exhausted around John; he just got me.

I had officially entered a real-life fantasy. We went out on lunch dates and romantic dinner dates together. I didn't even care if someone saw us. All I really cared about was myself, and I felt amazing! John evoked my beauty. He was so different from Charlie. He talked to me and listened to me. I wanted to divorce Charlie and be with John forever. I wanted the fantasy. I wanted to be rescued. I wanted to run away and leave everything I didn't want to face behind me. My pain had been masked by temporary happiness.

"I was dancing on top of a storm cloud so heavy with betrayal that it was only a matter of time until all hell broke loose."

-Me

A paralyzing reality hit me...I was a fraud, a liar, a cheater. *Oh my God, I was a cheater!* It was the very thing I had never wanted to be, the thing that had destroyed my childhood. It could not be true, I couldn't really have cheated on the man I'd said I would love forever. I held my head in my hands one night as I sat at the top of my stairs, sobbing in disbelief. My heart was racing inside of my body like a panicked, lost child. My thoughts ran in circles: *What have I done, what have I done? My marriage is destroyed, it's over! I have committed the ultimate betrayal.* I felt disgusting as I crawled back into bed beside Charlie. I was horrified. I couldn't sleep that night with my cardinal sin repeating in my mind again and again. If only I had just walked away that day in the park, if only I had been strong enough to say no. *If only, if only, if only…*. On and on and on I went in my head, driving myself crazy until finally I was so exhausted I fell into a deep sleep only to wake the next day with the truth broadcasting in my head: *"WHORE!"*

I was in complete denial that it was even my fault. I had been pushed to act this way—*right?* I had spoken my truth so many times and given Charlie every chance to change, and he hadn't. So of course it was his fault I'd taken my clothes off for someone else. I had prayed for this to happen a few months ago. I had prayed for someone else to come into my life and rescue me. I had told my husband this, he'd known I wasn't happy, he'd known I had prayed for someone else to find me. I had told him, and he had said nothing and done nothing, and I hated him for that. This was all his fault; he'd made me do this. He'd had his chance, he'd blown it, he didn't deserve me. I couldn't see the blame I was pushing onto him; my pain was too big. I justified my act of adultery so I could have an excuse to leave him, a reason to run from my own shadow. A darkness ran through my veins, and although my guilt was heavy and present every day, I let the affair continue. I was too selfish to end it.

We were fighting all the time, and between the fights we were barely talking. The days of not touching had turned into months. I needed to find leverage to leave, to build my case against him. I was a coward. I began to tell my parents about Charlie's drinking, trying to paint a picture of him that would justify my behavior. Everything I told them was true, but my intention was to manipulate them. I was hurting, so I wanted everyone to hurt with me. I agreed to go to counseling with him to keep up appearances even though I didn't give two shits about working on our marriage. I hated him even more by this point. I hated that it had taken him this long to care. I hated that I had told him over and over again of my unhappiness, trying to prevent this very outcome, and he hadn't heard me. I hated that I'd thought I had done everything my parents hadn't done before their divorce.

I pretended to care at the marriage counseling sessions we sat through together. I told the counselor that Charlie had a severe drinking problem, that he would drink and then drive home from his gigs every Saturday night. That he would come home drunk and start fights with me. That he would badger me and keep me up for hours, mentally and emotionally abusing me. All of this was true, but none of it was the truth. All of these reasons were only excuses so I could find what I was really seeking—myself. I pretended I wanted to work on our marriage, but secretly I was sleeping with another man the whole time. I was sitting in therapy and sleeping with someone else the whole fucking time.

I wanted to run away with John and start my life with him. But the truth remained that I was married and had two kids and was not free to do this. Months into the affair, I started getting worn out. The light that had turned on was dimming again. The excitement of the affair was wearing off, and I was starting to acknowledge my deep unhappiness. I realized that I didn't want John either. I had temporarily fallen in love with him, but I wasn't really in love with him. I didn't want the pain and scars of starting over in somebody else's life. I wanted my life, but I wanted it to look different, to be different. I called things off with John, crying in secret for weeks as my broken heart healed. I had been using John to find myself, a piece of me that I had lost along the way. He had brought a spark of beauty back into my life that I'd thought had died forever. I loved him for that. I left John, our friendship, and the chapter of us that I no longer wanted.

You could have cut the tension in the air with a knife the morning I looked Charlie in the eyes and confessed my emotional affair that had started six months earlier. I confessed my intimate affair that followed three months into the emotional affair. I confessed my unhappiness, my sorrow, and my conscious choice to experience something other than the agony I felt in being married. I felt the energy of the mountains pressing in on me as a clouded look of rage moved onto Charlie's face. Our morning hike had turned into my confessional, baring yet another layer of my naked soul. The color drained from the picture of our life as I told him everything. My choice hadn't solved anything, it had only hurt everyone, but you don't know until you know. What I had learned was how to feel beautiful again, how to dig deep and find my own strength in the darkness. I wasn't asking him to stay with me or like me or accept my choice. I was admitting to my own process, and I wanted to move forward. That day was awful for both of us. It was revealing and ugly. I felt like every thread of my being was exposed and every dark corner had been seen. I wasn't perfect. I'd had an affair.

We spent months trying to fix our broken hearts. We attended more counseling sessions. This time, I told the truth. I told the counselor I wasn't sorry for my choice because I'd made it consciously. I told her my heart was desperate and I'd found my beauty again. I told her Charlie had stood and said nothing when I'd told him what I had prayed for. My intention hadn't been to hurt Charlie, it had been to find myself. I realized I had done a lot of both. The counseling wasn't really working, I wasn't done discovering myself. I still felt my inner siren ringing deep inside of me. I could feel my sexual energy projecting outwardly in search of approval and validation. I still thought Charlie was an unsophisticated, overbearing asshole. I wanted my life back for comfort and to protect our children from experiencing pain, but not because I was in love with Charlie. Each attempt we made to work on us felt worse than the one before it. We went on disaster dates and made empty love to each other. He was no doubt replaying me fucking someone else over and over again in his head. I couldn't blame him for that. I had taken the innocence away from our relationship.

Knocking At My Door

Who's there? Yelling from my bed,
A voice inside my head.
Knocking, knocking at my door,
The voice increases even more.

Aching is the voice,
Hearing-not a choice.
Screaming in my head,
I'm yelling from my bed.

Go away, I am not here,
Search another, for I fear.
Go away and let me sleep,
Take the secrets that I keep.

For a moment silence breaks,
Then a force overtakes.
Screaming from my bed,
I'm yelling in my head.

First I look to only see
Something that will never be.
I am what you cannot see,
Bitter dreams of destiny.

But then a shadow moves,
My body-feeling bruised.
Dawn is in the sky,
My eyes-about to cry.

I'm still afraid to fall asleep
With the secrets that I keep.
Darkness falls all around,
Everywhere, without a sound.

Once again I hear the voice,
Every night, without a choice.
Knocking, knocking at my door,
The voice increases even more.

-Rosemarie

My Lesson: Betrayal

MY BETRAYAL WASN'T ONLY IN deceiving Charlie. My ultimate betrayal was in deceiving myself. I learned that taking shortcuts didn't take me any closer to creating true happiness. I realized through my affair that I had been damaged from my parents' divorce and never truly healed. I was living out of learned behavior and old conditioning. I had been a witness to unhappiness. I had been the silent observer of the loneliness and anger in their marriage that had led to an affair. I had watched the outward seeking of attention and the exhaustion of overworking in order to provide. I wanted to be different—I knew their behavior hadn't brought happiness—but I had already been conditioned. I learned that entering into another relationship while I was in a marriage offered nothing but pain. I wasn't in clean energy to truly be with someone else. I learned how unfair that choice was for me, for Charlie, and for John.

The Second Affair

alignment: a position of agreement or alliance

I NOTICED A NEW FACE IN the hallway of my building as I followed him down the stairway. I wasn't taking the elevator that day; there had been a sign taped across the silver door: "OUT OF ORDER!" So the stairs were my serendipitous option. It was leap day, February 29, 2016, a day that only exists every four years. It was a full year after my first affair had begun. As I stepped off the last stair and approached the stairway door, this stranger held it open for me. In an unusual gesture, he reached out and put both his arms around me, pulling me close to him as I stepped through the open doorway. He was embracing my body with his, intentionally hugging me. It felt like his entire energy had wrapped around every layer of mine. I honestly admit that I was startled by this unusual event but instantly intrigued. He was taller than me, so my face fell right at the curve of his neck. I was so close to him that I could easily smell his skin. It was captivating, and the combination of black amber and patchouli mixed with a soft tone of vanilla immediately got my attention. My senses were suddenly immersed in him. I made an awkward comment about how I liked his cologne and smiled as I walked away. He smiled back. My head was spinning—*What the hell was that?*

I could hear a piercing warning in the back of my head. Trouble was mounting the horizon because of that seemingly innocent hug. Over the next couple weeks, this stranger seemed to be everywhere. I ran into him in the hallway, on my way to the bathroom, and walking into my office building. Like magnets, we were energetically pulled together. I couldn't avoid him. Small talk ensued, personal questions were asked, a lingering stare was shared, and worst of all, the "friendly" flirtatious touching began. His hand would slowly caress the outside of my arm and trail down to my fingertips, pausing right at the curve of my hand before letting go completely. *Attraction!* It was a drug so powerful, I instantly felt alive.

You can imagine the thoughts that were running through my mind. *I can handle this. It's only flirting. I won't let this get out of control like last time. I have grown from my experience with John a year ago. I've got this!* I had taken time to practice what I would do if I was approached by another man. I would stand my ground and tell him I was happily married and that I appreciated the compliments and flirtations, but I was not available. I tried…I really tried. I stood stronger in more ways than I had during the first affair. I told him I was married and had two children and that we could only be friends. I did emphasize *friends* this time. But I did not say I was happily married, nor did I walk away feeling good about how I'd left the door wide open for our next encounter. And somehow, one day I ended up holding in my hand his phone number, written on a little slip of torn paper. I immediately felt regret, but it wasn't enough to stop me. I thought I could handle this, I thought I had control over myself this time. Why did the allure feel so good? I ran into him over and over again, and each time I gained more and more attraction for him. He was clearly interested in me, and certainly not as just a friend. Obviously, I wasn't questioning his motives; I was only interested in the high I felt every single time I saw him. A smarter version of me would have asked, *Why? Why the hell would a single, unmarried, childless, good-looking man want with a married mother of two struggling with a serious attention deficit disorder?* Universal law states that we attract those at the same level as ourselves.

I had a lot of work to do to unravel the deep patterning that I had been witness to as a child. The need for outside attention was completely sewn into my DNA, inherited like a predisposition to cancer. I had witnessed boredom and neglect and desperation for unconditional love. I was conditioned. I knew intimately the need to be seen and desired. I had been torn between two perspectives as a child—the fantasy of romance and the fantasy for easy, peaceful living. One was of great intensity and the other of fine simplicity. Neither was wrong, but both were confusing. My delicate observations had been seen through the undeveloped eyes of an innocent child, a child who didn't know the complexities of relationships. It had been an unfair position for an innocent observer.

Eventually, I admitted to myself that it was time to tell Charlie my newest and best idea ever: I wanted to see other people for the next six months. I told him I had met someone that I wanted to explore. I obviously wasn't very happy in our marriage, or someone else would not have gotten my attention again. I wanted an open relationship. I suggested it might be good for him, too, to have another experience with someone else.

He freaked out, of course. I mean, seriously, why would anyone in their right mind expect their partner to go for something that fucking crazy? Maybe I had seen too many movies. As you can see, I was so self-accommodating at this point that I had really expected him to be like, *Yeah, sure, honey, sounds like a great idea! Go ahead and fuck some new guy, and I'll be waiting right here when you're all done with him!* It dawned on me that I was truly sideways, and all the safety nets Charlie had offered me had to be removed so I could find my true path. I had to do it on my own. Finally, the crossroads had come, and I left. I couldn't take another day undercover; I wouldn't muster one more phony face to the world.

I moved out.

Letting Go

With each breath I breathe anew
I cleanse my world, I think of you

The world whispered in my ear
I heard it say, "Let go of FEAR"

I whispered back, "I'm not afraid"
It told me, "Life is like a braid

It twists and intertwines WITH TIME
Making stories out of mine"

I wondered, "Where would the braid go?"
The world said, "Stop and take it slow

There is a place that you will find
A place where you are no longer blind

The path will guide you there to SEE
Everything you are meant to BE"

As I think, I change my thoughts
Everything that I was taught.

Misbelief and hidden lies
I gather them and say goodbye.

I am mine, and mine alone
I choose my path, for me to own.

-Rosemarie

My Lesson: Addiction

OH, THE POWERFUL AND STRANGE allure of addiction. Charlie was addicted to alcohol, but I was an addict, too. I had a strong addiction for attention, the seductive feeling of being important enough to obtain another's interest. This addiction was the stimulus for the inappropriate behavior that caused deliberate drama in my life. It had a serious hold on me, and just as the last hit of heroin can take you down, so can a final, deadly attraction. I learned that addiction doesn't play favorites; it takes anyone who has a weakness. It wraps you up in deceit and plays your soul like a little bitch.

The Separation

seperation: cessation of cohabitation between a married couple by mutual agreement or judicial decree

THE NEXT FEW MONTHS WERE tough. I had no idea how hard the separation would be on the kids—and on my heart. It was awful. I would tuck them into a shared bottom bunk every night in their new room because they didn't feel safe enough to sleep alone. Every night they would ask me why I didn't love Daddy anymore and why I'd left him, and they would just cry. It broke me up inside. The worst night was when my daughter told me I had ruined her "perfect," that her life would never be the same, and she hated me for that. I couldn't explain to them why I needed what I needed. I could only love them through their sadness. I hadn't considered all the pain the kids would be feeling from their perfect little world being torn apart. I hadn't thought about how much I would miss them on the weeks they were at their dad's house. I missed them tremendously, and I missed Charlie too—I missed being a family. I hadn't considered that Charlie would be crying with them in our bed, cuddling them to sleep every night in agony. Or that his heart would be broken, and the kids would be witnesses to his horrific heartache. I had been so wrapped up in my own anger, I hadn't thought of anyone but myself.

To elude my madness, I found myself working as much as I could. My little office offered a refuge to escape my current reality and focus on my clients. The teal velvet couches were a reminder of my clients' stories and how I wasn't the only one going through something difficult.

My other outlet was running through the expansive desert landscape. The feeling of my feet hitting the sandy earth allowed me to let go and breathe. The earth never judged me. The desert was there to heal me. It was my truest friend. I would run to the same spot every time. There, I would throw my arms up toward the sky and exclaim, "I love you!" I would often cry at that spot in the desert as I offered my heart to the Universe. I asked for peace and guidance. I surrendered my anger there. I asked the Universe to give me eyes to see and ears to hear. The desert filled my soul enough so that I could go on every day. I did better if my schedule was occupied; work, exercise, and meditation were all outlets so I didn't have to feel the pain of being alone. It sucked.

My biggest illusion was in thinking I'd needed total independence from Charlie in order to be myself. I'd left my husband, children, home, and life and moved into a small isolated apartment alone. I saw my children every other week. I paid all my own bills, slept by myself, made decisions by myself, and ate by myself. I could come and go as I pleased, and at first I felt courageous—everything was exciting. But as time crept along, I began to realize that Charlie had never been my prison. I had enslaved myself. I had created the idea that I wasn't independent, I had created the falsity that his behavior was somehow a reflection of me. But it wasn't; he was his own reflection. I had blamed him because I had been too ashamed to see my reflection. I had been weak, and I had been a coward. I hadn't had enough self-love and self-worth while in the marriage to see this. I hadn't been able to see anything until I was alone and loving myself.

"In order to create a new consciousness, time must be spent weeding the garden of the mind."

-Me

I spent six months in my little apartment figuring it all out. I cried a lot, journaled, meditated, worked a ton, dated, and walked in the desert and contemplated my thoughts, beliefs, and conditioning. It was an uncertain and challenging time. I had ups and downs in my self-discovery. I knew I had to dig deep and really circumnavigate everything about myself in order to come out of this with a renewed perspective. It felt good to take the time I needed to get to know myself after years of staying at home and raising a family. I took the time I needed to rediscover myself as a woman. I was privileged to have been able to care for my kids every day until they went to school, but I couldn't have predicted how lost I would become through that experience. Caretaking is a full-time job with very little recognition. It is tiring and often unfulfilling. Constantly caring for others' needs completely depleted my energy. I had forgotten myself along the way; I had forgotten the vivacious, free-spirited beauty that I was.

The way I feel about you...(me)

I love the way you care for me, the special time you take
You make me feel so beautiful, like frosting on a cake
I love the way you love me, how you talk to me so fine
I love how nice you are to me, I love that you are mine
You never put me down, not to anyone we know
Your words are always loving, only beauty do you sow
I love the way you encourage me to be my very best
How you always give me stickers on every single test!
I love the way you listen, how you hear my inner voice
How you never interrupt me and always give me a choice
You love with pure intention, a light that shines right through
You are my greatest sunrise and most magic sunset, too
I love the way you see me like a mermaid floating by
I am your constant captivation, your personal Mai Tie
I cherish and adore you, my dearest, truest friend
You love me like no other, a love that never ends!

-Rosemarie

My Lesson: Reprogramming

MY "TIME OUT" GAVE ME the space I needed and enough heartache to get down and dirty with myself. I spent hours connecting with my inner soul, addressing my old conditioning, learning how to think differently, and replacing my shadows with new awareness. I identified the patterns I had been living out that weren't even mine. I discovered what I liked and how to be okay with what I liked. I found my voice and learned how to speak with truth. I forgave myself for letting others influence me so much, and I forgave myself for not knowing what I didn't know until I knew it. I found everything I needed right inside of me, right where it had been waiting the whole time. I was finally worth getting to know, and I was falling head over heels in love with myself!

The Divorce

divorce: dissolving a union in which you are no longer aligned

YOU CAN'T POSSIBLY UNDERSTAND DIVORCE until you have gone through the absolute trauma of dissolving a family. You spend countless hours thinking about divorce. You run scenarios over and over again in your mind, justifying, contemplating, exhausting yourself over and over until you call a lawyer, draw up the paperwork, and start the dreaded legal process. It's nothing short of a nightmare even in the most cordial and peaceful cases. Inviting the legal system into your life through mediation and court hearings is a violation. Having a judge decide how your precious children will spend their parent time is daunting, and having to be connected to that system until they are eighteen is overwhelming. Splitting up is like a funeral that doesn't end. The array of feelings is a tireless cycle of repetition. Normal escalates to fury, peaks in resentment, calms back down to normal, and then the whole fucking cycle repeats itself. But all the while, you would rather rinse and repeat your own turmoil than allow the other person to win.

Then, on top of all that drama, you start thinking you are ready to date when you haven't even completed the relationship you are in. Then you start thinking about your kids spending time with the stranger your ex is dating, whom you know nothing about. All the while, you're getting letters from pissed-off relatives about how you are ruining your life and the lives of your children. You are seeing fear emerge in people you have known forever, your friends are choosing sides and having nasty exchanges, you're feeling unsupported by your own parents, you're crying alone and often, you're experiencing bursts of feeling free but more often sleepless nights, and all the while you're rationalizing, blaming, renegotiating, pleading, begging, crying more, having meaningless sex with people, and jumping into new relationships to ease the pain of being left, cheated on, betrayed, and unheard. These are all part of the hideous process of divorce.

I was sitting on the plane heading to LA with my newest boyfriend James. I had lied to Charlie about what I was doing. He thought I was visiting my longtime girlfriend for the weekend. I lied because it was easier than telling him the truth. I lied because I didn't want to hurt him. I lied because he had a girlfriend, and I was tired of his lies. I lied because I didn't owe him anything anymore. I lied knowing we had been getting along better than ever the week before. I lied because maybe it wasn't over between us. I told him that I needed a couple of weeks to sort out my shit. I figured he did too, considering he had a girlfriend and had agreed. I knew he still loved me, and I gave him hope.

But I went on the trip with James anyway. I wanted to go—I had to know for sure I wasn't making the wrong decision if I broke it off with him. Charlie and I had been separated for eight months, and a lot of dirty water was flowing under our bridge. The thought of getting back together with him and that being a mistake terrified me. James moved closer to me as I showed him a picture of Charlie. I had assumed he already knew what Charlie looked like; everyone I knew in the dating world did immediate online searches. He said he hadn't looked him up, and I could tell by his expression that he was shocked by Charlie's appearance. James had a bigger-than-life personality and didn't hide his thoughts or emotions. He blurted out, "Why are you giving that up?" It caught me by surprise, and by the time I glanced up at him, he had already looked away. My inner thought was, *Yeah, why am I giving that up?*

By the time I landed back in Phoenix, Charlie was losing his mind. He must have called me a hundred times and left irate messages. He had found out I hadn't been at my girlfriend's house, and he was furious. This was the tantrum I had been trying to avoid. When I finally got to the house to pick up the kids, he told me it was over, that he wanted the divorce papers submitted on Monday morning. He was devastated. I had hurt him again.

The divorce paperwork was submitted first thing Monday morning. I cried a million tears that morning in my car before I left the courthouse. I could feel my heart fracturing in all directions. Would I ever heal? Memory after memory stormed my mind as I sobbed and hyperventilated. I was sitting alone in my little black car, watching Charlie walk across the parking lot away from me. It was over. My life with Charlie as I'd known it was over. Our diseased, conditioned, desperate, addictive, disappointing relationship of betrayal had ended, completing lifetimes of unfinished business. Divorced. One contract had ended, and a new one would begin.

"From one lifetime to another, we serve each other."

-Me

Divorce

Seven suns, and I wonder
"Should I stay or should I go?"
This place is drowning under
The home I used to know

The crying of the Angels
The breaking of our Love
Time has slowly whispered
"Fly away, my little dove!"

Where is the sanctity of marriage
In our modern-day court?
Innocent precious children
Asking, "Which parent will I abort?"

The overwhelming sadness
Each tear that falls, the truth
Of a family once established
And now beyond all cuth.

But with each love that ends
A new begins to bloom
The story starts its chapter
And life, it does resume.

-Rosemarie

My Lesson: Ending Cycles

I LEARNED THAT IT'S OKAY TO end cycles that no longer serve you. We spend lifetimes in relationships with others working on our lessons together. I realized that Charlie helped me break old cycles that no longer served me. I understood that coming from betrayal in our own families had left us with a predisposition for divorce. Dissolving an agreement that had been made with a conditioned understanding gave us freedom to choose something new. We were empowered to create our lives from a healthy perspective, washed clean of the lies we had been taught and were witness to. I was truly learning how to love from a place free of conditioning, a place I wanted to move further into, a place of unconditional love!

A New Beginning

unconditional love: an affection without any limitations, or love without conditions, or complete love

IT WAS A WEEK BEFORE Christmas 2016 and two full years since I had sent out my emergency 911 prayer to the Universe. I could have never imagined then the journey I would take after desperately making that call.

Charlie reached across the table to hold my hand. The children looked at each other in confusion when we told them that we were going to be spending the holidays together. Their little faces lit up with sheer joy that brought instant tears to my eyes. Months of their broken hearts had been restored in a simple sentence. It was a contagious flash of happiness. The memory of my brother and I sitting at our dining room table the day our parents told us the saddest truth suddenly came back to me. I had come full circle. My brother and I never had a second chance as a family, but the hands that joined together that day did! We weren't done; in fact, we were just getting started.

I kept my apartment until the end of May, when my lease was up. I didn't want there to be any pressure on Charlie and I as we built a new foundation together. We had both ended our relationships with other people and cleaned up our contacts. We cleared out our phones of old messages, emails, and texts. To be honest, I was so exhausted from our two-year crisis that another person was the last thing on my mind. All I wanted was to be with my family and rest. I wanted to be with the family that I had created, with a man who wasn't perfect, who still had work to do, but was mine. In our own little nuclear family, we had each other for the good, the bad, and the ugly.

We decided not to share with each other every naked detail of what we had experienced during our separation. Whatever had happened to Charlie through his encounters had changed him for the better. I felt deep gratitude for any other women who had played a role in his life during that time. I felt like he had reached a more present and evolved state of being from his experiences.

Charlie hadn't given up drinking yet, and he had actually started smoking during our spilt. An old habit, I suppose, that took the sting of lonely nights away. I didn't care; I knew we were rehabbing, and unconditional love was now my main focus. No more telling him what to do or being passive aggressive or making his behavior about me. No, it was time for a true practice of unconditional love—may it shine its light through me! I had made a new declaration to the Universe: "Help me to love Charlie from the place that the Universe loves me from."

> "The Universe never says, 'Why don't you love and support me?' It only says, 'How can I love and support you?'"
>
> -Me

I was done being needy and making Charlie's pain about how he didn't love me enough to choose me over alcohol. I didn't care if he chose me or not anymore; I was choosing him.

Things were slow at first. We were both learning how to trust each other again. "Sex" and "Money" are always the winners in building trust. Our intimacy was gentle and allowing as we merged our energies back together. It felt like home, like being with him was where I belonged. He was a perfect fit. We kept finances separate, and that felt healthy. In our old relationship, everything was mixed together, and we had no freedom to manage our money in our own individual ways. Charlie had come around a lot in the finance area. He had learned how to budget his own books, and he had received a raise at work, freeing him up to make some new choices for himself and for us. It felt good, and I loved being the witness to new aspects of this man, who had become a brighter, bigger, more confident version of his previous self.

The sprawling green landscape of England was the perfect family holiday that summer. It was like a dream to be there all together. The rain sprinkled down on us as we marched around the sacred grounds at Stonehenge. The rocks stacked up like keys set in the earth, making a mystical portal into another dimension. Life took a pause as we meandered up and down the quaint streets of Windsor, Canterbury, and Norfolk, popping in and out of all the little shops, collecting trinkets of all sorts. We drank cups of tea with relatives, chatted for hours, had pints at the pub, and enjoyed every minute we spent together. Being there as a family made me feel like I had stolen something back from the dead. I felt as if we'd had a do-over. I considered myself the luckiest person to have been blessed with a second chance at being a family.

2017 moved fast after that vacation. Charlie played gigs on Saturday nights. His drinking had calmed somewhat, but there was still the occasional drunken tantrum. They seemed to be further and further apart from each other. He had given up smoking and was making obvious progress. I still felt flares of my old "fix, manage, and control" personality pattern. I wanted more than anything to not project "me" onto Charlie. Ultimately, I needed more surrender. I was practicing with devotion to not take his choices personally, and I was getting better over time.

I noticed Charlie changing more and more over the next

year. His former self was dying. A new consciousness was being born. We were having deep conversations about our childhoods and our conditioning from our parents. An awareness started to emerge within Charlie, a personal awakening. I saw in him a new authority that was beginning to transform how he wanted to live his life, a desire to let go of how he had been taught to do things, and a new freedom to choose for himself. At times, he struggled to believe that the pain he was holding onto was holding him back and affecting his life as a grown-up. It takes courage to address the past, and I was watching Charlie let go inch by inch.

> *"I am a collection of conditionings. It is my responsibility to dissolve any conditioning that no longer serves me."*
>
> *-Me*

We had decided to renovate the entire downstairs of our home. It was already the summer of 2018, and we were managing life together really well. I felt comfortable with a remodel and the expense of it. It was a big commitment and would displace us from our home for an entire month. My mom's empty vacation home served as our refuge until the project completed in mid-August.

We had made it to the final week of the project when the pressure took over. It had been a normal Saturday together: laughing, talking, playing with the kids, and Charlie's usual packing up of the car with music equipment for his gig that evening. I had plans to have dinner with the kids and friends that night. It was business as usual. Louis and Rosebud had so much fun playing with my girlfriend's children that they asked to sleep over. I returned to our temporary place alone that evening and waited for Charlie to get home. I hopped in the shower to clean up from my day, brushed my teeth, and crawled into bed, hoping he would be home soon. The black night swallowed me up into slumber; I fell asleep.

I woke at the noise of keys fumbling in the keyhole and the loud cursing that came from the other side of the door. Charlie had finally arrived home close to midnight. With a frustrated push—he was having great trouble getting through the front door—the door swung open. I'd gotten out of bed and watched him stumble and fall through the entryway. At first, I thought he had tripped over the threshold, but it only took me seconds to recognize that familiar drunken slur and body language. He was totally fucking wasted! My mind was racing with questions I didn't ask: *Did you wreck the car on the way home? Was there a hit-and-run? Did you hurt anyone else?* All my greatest fears mounted quickly on top of each other. I looked at him with a steady gaze as the pit of my stomach fell to the floor. This was my ultimate test. How would I choose to love him in this moment? I could have yelled at him, provoked him, told him that it was over between us—all the things I had done before. But I didn't. I chose to love him fiercely that night. I didn't throw anything in his face; in fact, I did the opposite. As if stroking a cat in the wrong direction, I listened to his drunken nonsense and told him that I loved him.

Charlie passed out the moment his body hit the bed. His breaths were heavy as I silently acknowledged that I had done something different. I had arrived at a new location with Charlie, a place I had never ventured before. I had made a new choice. I had changed my formula! The following morning, Charlie was embarrassed and remorseful. He could barely look at my face and couldn't remember the details from the night before. I told Charlie that I loved him, that I supported him, that I wasn't leaving him. I told him I was his partner and he was mine through thick and thin. I told him that as his friend, however, I had a responsibility to tell him he might want to consider getting his shit together. I kissed him on the forehead and left to pick up the kids.

It wasn't long after that final drunken tantrum that Charlie approached me. He cried and confessed that he had made a terrible decision that night when he drove home. He didn't remember driving home that evening. He felt like the Universe had saved him one final time and given him an opportunity to make a change. He thanked me for not scolding him or making him feel bad about himself. He told me I had shown up differently for him that night, and he had noticed. He confided that he was done drinking.

I had been waiting a long time to hear Charlie say this. I found it fascinating that it took doing the exact opposite of what I had always done in order for it to happen.

"Change your formula, change your outcome!" No truer statement can be found in the history of human existence!

Maybe I could have had a different relationship a long time ago with Charlie had I chosen unconditional love sooner. Hindsight is always twenty-twenty. Looking back can only help you move forward. That is what we were doing together as a team, no longer in competition of whose painful story was worth more. Both stories were equally awful, and we didn't need trophies to prove it. We only wanted to move into a life that accepted where we had come from but didn't define who we were becoming.

Our house turned out beautifully. We settled back into a newly refreshed home. The remodel included new floors and baseboards, a beautiful, cascading, gray-veined, white-quartz waterfall island, fresh paint, and reconfigured walls. I was in love. New energy was swirling around our house like a swarm of yellow butterflies.

I looked out our dining room window to see Charlie once again standing in his Zen meditation garden. He had built this sanctuary after letting go of drinking. It was a place of solitude for him to reflect and listen. He had planted vegetables that were already sprouting to life. Hose in hand, he watered them like clockwork every morning and every night. He was symbolically creating life as he grew his own. The garden was life that he was responsible for, life that relied on him to thrive. He was experiencing a sense of peace, a place of surrender. I loved watching him in his garden.

I could see that it was the way the Universe was drawing him home.

I felt like I was in some kind of alternative reality with Charlie. *Pinch me! Can this really be my life? Can the man I had hated two short years ago truly be the man I am in love with today?* I know it seems impossible, but it happened. I don't know where life will take me in the future—how can anyone really know? What I do know is I found peace buried in the deep recesses of my soul. Peace that no one can take from me. I found myself. As ugly as the job was, I undressed Her.

Somewhere

I have arrived somewhere
And I am not late
I have arrived right here
My perfect fate

I went backwards, and forwards
And upside down
Only to see myself
Flat on the ground

Forwards and backwards
I spun, and I turned
Over and under
To see what I learned

Over and under
I flipped all around
I twisted and turned
to see what I found

Backwards and forwards
I see myself go
Over and under
I finally know

I have arrived somewhere
And I am not late
I have arrived right here
My perfect fate

-Rosemarie

My Lesson: Gratitude

I LEARNED THAT GRATITUDE BREEDS GOODNESS. It is the magic ingredient to all change! In order for me to have more, I needed to be able to appreciate what I already had. I learned that it is better to be kind than right, and there is nothing attractive about being a victim. I learned that love with conditions is toxic. I learned that I am enough, that I am unconditionally loved and never alone. All along the way I _asked_, I _surrendered_, and I _listened_ to the Universe as it guided me. The whole time, even in the darkest alleys of my discoveries, I knew who I worked for and who was working for me. In the mystery of it all, I found TRUE UNCONDITIONAL LOVE!

-Thank you

Epilogue

"She said yes, and so did he, not even knowing what was meant to be. Each had a past that had scarred their skin; they were two young souls with conditioning."

I CAME FROM A FAMILY OF four. A standard American family with a standard American story: boy meets girl, they fall in love, boy asks girl to marry him, girl gets pregnant shortly after wedding, they have a baby girl (me), and two years later they have a boy (my little brother). My mom stayed home to raise us while my dad worked hard to provide for us. This was the standard and completely typical of the small town I was born in. In fact, for a family to be anything other than that was abnormal. My mom grew up in England with an alcoholic father and an inattentive mother whom she claims provided her with absolutely no attention whatsoever. My dad had a sweet subservient mother and an overly strict father who at times used physical discipline. Both my parents liked to drink and party on occasion, and both seemed to love us very much. I always felt wanted. Somewhere around my fourteenth birthday, my parents sat us down and told us they were getting a divorce. There had been an affair and a hardening of their hearts. I felt abandonment creep in along with anger, sadness, betrayal, and resentment. Charlie should have seen the writing on the wall stating that I was completely fucked up when he met me. His wedding vows should have went:

"I take this broken girl to be my wife in her sickness of betrayal and abandonment, to

> have and to hold while at some point during
> our marriage she will most likely have a total
> fucking meltdown resulting in an affair. She
> will most likely choose someone much older
> than her so she can deal with her undeveloped
> self-worth. No problem at all, I've got this."

Charlie came from a dysfunctional family of seven with a less traditional story: girl meets boy with ex-wife and young son, they fall in love and get married. Charlie's mom came from a traditional fifties household where the mom wore the apron and the dad laid down the law. Charlie's dad's dad was an unavailable alcoholic who died young, after which his dad's mother married a man thirty years her junior. This left Charlie with an emotionally abused homemaker, an unfaithful and emotionally abusive alcoholic, a half-brother from his dad's previous marriage, twin brothers—one of whom died at seventeen in the woods behind their house in a hunting accident—and finally a little brother, with whom Charlie shared a birthday as they had been born on the same day three years apart. Divorce ensued. Charlie's parents split when he was sixteen, leaving him to grow up without proper supervision or guidance. Partying and drinking soon followed. If I were to really have looked at this painful family, I would have recognized the absolute pain, sorrow, loss, resentment, anger, fear, lies, betrayal, and abandonment. I would have known that I was marrying a man with wounds so deep they may never heal. I would have incorporated in my wedding vows the following:

> "I take this man in his horror, in his corrupt
> conditioning of love, in his sadness and pain,
> in faith that God will work that shit out with
> him. I am totally aware that he will most likely
> be an angry emotional alcoholic who hates
> confrontation and does anything to hide his

true feelings. Sure, I can endure years and years of this incredibly frustrating behavior. I've got this!"

Our marriage story was the result of our families' betrayal and abandonment. We both came from families that had experienced deep pain and resentment. We had come together to heal the wounds that we hadn't even created but had received through the conditioning of others. We were on a mission to see the world with clear eyes. We were two young people with bags so heavy, we would inevitably drop them at some point in our relationship. We were like fireflies drawn to the fire and enchanted by the other. We would have the opportunity to heal the wounds that had been so deeply carved throughout our tender childhood years.

"I have chosen this exact life, my death will come after I have fulfilled my mission!"
                                                              -Me

Printed in the United States
By Bookmasters